SANCTIFIED F.R.E.A.K.

Dr. Vicki Tyler Waters

Sanctified

F.R.E.A.K.

God, Marriage, And Sexual Intimacy

Sanctified F.R.E.A.K.
Dr. Vicki Tyler Waters
Cover Design by Koa Publishing Company

Published by Koa Publishing Company
A Division of
Koa Publishing Company and Mommy Bee Books For Young
Learners, LLC
Manassas, VA 20109
www.koapublishingcompany.com

Library of Congress
Copyright © 2024 Dr. Vicki Tyler Waters
ISBN 979-8-9860577-6-7

Printed in the United States of America

DEDICATION

I dedicate this book to my best friend who just so happens to be my husband. Ray, you have been such an encouragement to me ever since the day we first met. You have supported, loved, challenged, and believed in me. You have allowed me to be who God created me to be and have fully accepted the calling that God has on my life. You have never made me feel that I needed to walk behind you. Instead, you have made me feel that it is an honor for you to walk beside me. You are truly living up to your motto of just wanting to be the best follower of Jesus that you can be. Thank you for constantly praying for me and covering every area of my life. Thank you for honoring me not only as your wife but also your sister in Christ. You truly are a Man(d) of God. 😊

GIVING HONOR

A special thanks to two people who have truly impacted my life and have been instrumental in my growth and in the completion of this book:

Pastor William Derricott Jr.

If there were pictures in the dictionary, your face would be beside the word *cheerleader*. You have been one of my biggest cheerleaders. You have encouraged, challenged, and believed in me. You saw things in me that I didn't see in myself. You and Pastor Key were the first ones, outside of our church, to fully embrace our marriage ministry and especially the part dealing with sexual intimacy. You both believed in us and because of that, many doors have been opened to us for ministry. You are the one that I call when I have something to share, whether it was a revelation or something great that God has done. I can always depend on you to respond with an amazed "WOW" an encouraging word, or you telling me that I just, "Made your baby leap". Thank you!

Apostle Myrtle Johnson

In the book, "The 8th Habit". Stephen Covey states that a leader is someone who has the ability to see the potential or worth in something or someone and be able to express that to the person in such a way that not only does the person believe it, but they also act upon it (this is paraphrased. You have been that leader/mentor for me since we first met. You also have challenged, corrected, and loved me. Like the old saying goes, Love without truth is hypocrisy, truth without love is brutal. Give the truth in love. I am beyond blessed to call you my Mentor. Thank you!

CONTENTS

INTRODUCTION
WHY DID I WRITE THIS BOOK

I never would have imagined in a million years that I would write a book about sexual intimacy in marriage, especially for those who are believers in Jesus Christ. Sexual intimacy in marriage is not something that is regularly taught in church. I once heard someone say that there are two things that people don't want to talk about in church, sex and money, but they want them both. Why is sex, to some believers a taboo subject? It certainly is everywhere. You can't turn on the tv, radio or social media without someone talking about sex, having sex, complaining about sex or wanting sex. Sex is one of those topics that generate all types of emotions but is still woven into the fabric of all of our lives.

The church is a place where we can learn and grow. In the right setting at the right place at the right time, the topic of sex can be discussed in a wholesome and healthy way. God never intended for sex to be seen as cheap, dirty, illicit, tawdry or as a means of controlling someone or just to fulfill a physical or emotional need.

Paraphrasing a well known rapper, "A Lady publicly but a freak in bed". My question is, how many of us believers agreed with that statement, were offended by that statement or totally disagreed with that statement? I have to admit that when I first heard the song, there was no emotional response but I remembered that particular line because the song also had a catchy tune.

What does it mean to be a "freak" in the bed? Is it sacrilegious to think that a Christian can be a freak in the bed and still glorify God? I am so glad you asked those questions. My vision for this book is to open your eyes to see that a Christian can be both saved and totally free in the bedroom.

DISCLAIMER

I promise you that this is not a book on how to have sex, where to have sex, participating in all kinds of sex in all kinds of places and in all kinds of ways. This is not an instructional book or a step by step guide to great sex. This is a book about romantic love between a husband and wife and to encourage you to enjoy the gift from God of sexual intimacy, God's way.

F- Free
R- Righteous
E- Engaging
A- Accessible
K- Knowledgeable

Part I

What is a Sanctified F.R.E.A.K.?

CHAPTER 1
FREE

Free- *not under the control or in the power of another*

I heard someone say that we should not allow our past to hold our future hostage. As Christians we all have a past. We all have made some bad choices and decisions that we wish we would not have made. Some of us have gotten caught up with the wrong person and did things that we wish we would not have done. I'm referring to consensual sexual encounters or relationships involving sex. These kinds of premarital or extramarital activities can have lasting impacts on the individual or married couple's sexual, spiritual, and emotional (soul) well-being.

As in any sexual or even nonsexual relationship, the experience will leave a type of "footprint" on your life. These "footprints" are the impressions, markings or images left in a person's soul. They are invisible connections, often referred to as a "soul tie". What's worse is if the sex was nonconsensual, the soul tie will also be created as the result of joined bodies. In such cases, the affected individual may experience flashes of bad memories, blacked out memories, and bodily stress from physical trauma. There is also shame, guilt, and other emotional reactions.

Years ago, many members of our church attended a soul cleansing/deliverance retreat and there they conducted a demonstration of something called, "The Path to Purity". This demonstration showed what happens when a man and woman get married and how through that union, they bring past sexual partners into their bedroom. For example, John marries Jill and they both have had multiple sexual partners and experiences. The diagram on the next page shows what that could possibly look like, making some moderate assumptions on behavior.

Soul Tie For Two or More?

Take a look at one ex partner or experience on each level.

Koa Publishing Company 2023

So, when John and Jill come together sexually, they both bring all the people that they have ever had a sexual relationship with into their bedroom-feelings, emotions, experiences. This is not meant to bring about condemnation but to bring understanding on how other sexual partners can impact your married life.

Here is the good news according to the Word of God in Romans, Chapter 8:1-11

"Therefore, there is now no condemnation for those who are in Christ Jesus, because through Christ Jesus the law of the Spirit who gives life has set you free from the law of sin and death. For what the law was powerless to do because it was weakened by the flesh, God did by sending his own Son in the likeness of sinful flesh to be a sin offering. And so, he condemned sin in the flesh, in order that the righteous requirement of the law might be fully met in us, who do not live according to the flesh but according to the Spirit. Those who live according to the flesh have their minds set on what the flesh desires; but those who live in accordance with the Spirit have their minds set on what the Spirit desires. The mind governed by the flesh is death, but the mind governed by the Spirit is life and peace. The mind governed by the flesh is hostile to God; it does not submit to God's law, nor can it do so. Those who are in the realm of the flesh cannot please God. You, however, are not in the realm of the flesh but are in the realm of the Spirit, if indeed the Spirit of God lives in you. And if anyone does not have the Spirit of Christ, they do not belong to Christ. But if Christ is in you, then even though your body is subject to death because of sin, the Spirit gives life because of

righteousness. And if the Spirit of him who raised Jesus from the dead is living in you, he who raised Christ from the dead will also give life to your mortal bodies because of his Spirit who lives in you."

2nd Corinthians 5:17
"Therefore, if anyone is in Christ, the new creation has come: The old has gone, the new is here." And in John 8:36 *"So if the Son sets you free, you will be free indeed."*

1st John 1:9
"If we confess our sins, he is faithful and just and will forgive us our sins and purify us from all unrighteousness."

There is true freedom from your past. Jesus paid the ultimate price for your freedom, now walk in it.

Reflections
As I conclude this first chapter, think about what it means to be free sexually in your marriage. Then ask yourself the following questions and answer them honestly.

1. How has your past relationships impacted your marriage?

2. Are you still living in the past with a lot of regrets?
3. How did you feel when you saw the diagram about soul ties?
4. Have you been able to forgive yourself for past sins?
5. What is your biggest takeaway from reading this first chapter?

Prayer

Father, in Jesus name please forgive me for all of my sins and cleanse me from all unrighteousness. I break every soul tie and bond between me and everyone that I engaged in sexual intercourse with outside of marriage. I will walk in freedom from my past and move onto more freedom in marriage now or when I get married. I will no longer allow the enemy to bombard my mind with impure sexual thoughts, past relationships and I will no longer walk in guilt and shame. I am cleansed through and by the blood of Jesus.

CHAPTER 2
RIGHTEOUS

Righteous- *acting in accord with divine or moral law*

Righteous is a strange word to use when you are talking about sex. How many of us think of sex as a righteous act or even a spiritual behavior? We usually define sex as a physical act between two individuals. However, people have sex for various reasons. Heck, there are people who pay to have sex with someone else. In these cases, this is not about a bond or covenant but simply a need or desire being met. However, in the bible sex is taught as an act of a covenant relationship between a husband and wife. 1st Corinthians 7:1-7

Now for the matters you wrote about: "It is good for a man not to have sexual relations with a woman." [2] But since sexual immorality is occurring, each man should have sexual relations with his own wife, and each woman with her own husband. [3] The husband should fulfill his marital duty to his wife, and likewise the wife to her husband. [4] The wife does not have authority over her own body but yields it to her husband. In the same way, the husband does not have authority over his own body but yields it to his wife. [5] Do not deprive each other except perhaps by mutual consent and for a time, so that you may devote yourselves to prayer. Then come together again so that Satan will not tempt you because of your lack of self-control. [6] I say this as a concession, not as a command. [7] I wish that all of you were as I am. But each of you has your own gift from God; one has this gift, another has that.

Some may have a problem with the "Wife/husband does not have authority over their body but the spouse does." In my opinion this does not mean that neither the husband nor wife has a say concerning their body but that in a marriage covenant, the wife should freely give of her body to her husband and the husband should freely give of his body to his wife. I believe in this area of marriage, open communication is key. A husband and wife should openly talk to each other about their wants and desires. I also believe that this is something that should be discussed prior to getting married (maybe with a marriage counselor) basically discussing expectations of each other.

I believe a spouse should not have to beg, plead, or barter when it comes to sexual intimacy. It should be a time of mutual consent where each spouse gives, receives and fully enjoy each other. I believe that God not only created sex as a way of producing children but also a time of a husband and wife coming together to unite in spirit, soul, and body. I remember a well-known pastor teaching the importance of praying together before sexual intimacy. Who would have ever thought that you could ask God to bless your sexual intimacy.

If you pray about health, finances, work, etc., why not pray and ask God to bless your time together; that it will be mutually satisfying, that both husband and wife's desires are met. The great part about marital sexual intimacy is that you are in it together. You not only share a bed, but you also share a room, a house, and you share each other's lives.

Reflections

Consider the righteousness of marital sex and intimacy. Answer the following questions as a check up on your knowledge, beliefs, and awareness of God's involvement.

1. Have you ever viewed sexual intimacy as a righteous act?
2. Do you think of your marriage as a spiritual covenant?

3. Have you attended a church where they talked about sexual intimacy?
4. Have you and your spouse ever prayed before having sexual intimacy?
5. What is your biggest takeaway from reading this chapter?

Prayer
Father, please forgive me for the times I have deliberately withheld my body from my spouse. Forgive me of the times that I did not take his/her desires into consideration. Please help me to see that making love with my spouse is a righteous act and that it honors you because it is in obedience to your word. Help me to keep prayer at the forefront of my life and help me to seek you when I feel tired, weary, unattractive, unlovable, etc. I understand that marital sexual intimacy is a gift from God and is not something to be seen as a chore but a blessing.

CHAPTER 3
ENGAGING

Engaging- *participate or become involved in*

"How you view it, is how you do it", Marital sexual intimacy should not be viewed as a chore or obligation. For some of us, our past is still dictating our personal life. Like me, some of us were not virgins when we married and some of us had bad sexual experiences such as abuse or being forced to engage in sexual activity and therefore was not a willing participant. I totally understand that these experiences were a violation of you and your body. God wants you to give these experiences to him so that he can heal you to be all he created you to be in every area of life… not just sexual intimacy.

As stated in Chapter 1, the price has been paid for your freedom in every area of life. You can freely give yourself to your spouse and be free to express that love not as an obligation but a privilege and an honor. You truly can be naked and not ashamed. I believe that the best marital sexual intimacy occurs when both spouses are full engaged, free to explore, playful, sensual, supportive, talkative and expressive. I also think that it is important that each spouse take turns initiating sexual intimacy. You can be free in the bedroom or wherever you decide to be together.

Hebrews 13:4
"Marriage should be honored by all, and the marriage bed kept pure, for God will judge the adulterer and all the sexually immoral."

There is nothing wrong with exploring each other's body. I believe that all five senses should be fully alive while making love: taste, touch, smell, sight, and hearing. For example, read the excerpt below from the Song of Solomon:

Chapter 4:
[1] How beautiful are you, my darling! Oh, how beautiful! Your eyes behind your veil are doves. Your hair is like a flock of goats descending from the hills of Gilead. [2]Your teeth are like a flock of sheep just shorn, coming up from the washing. Each has its twin; none of them is alone. [3] Your lips are like a scarlet ribbon; your mouth is lovely. Your temples behind your veil are like the halves of a pomegranate. [4] Your

neck is like the tower of David, built with courses of stone on it hang a thousand shields, all of them shields of warriors. ⁵ Your breasts are like two fawns, like twin fawns of a gazelle that browse among the lilies. ⁶ Until the day breaks and the shadows flee; I will go to the mountain of myrrh and to the hill of incense. ⁷ You are altogether beautiful, my darling; there is no flaw in you.

Chapter 5:

¹⁰My beloved is radiant and ruddy, outstanding among ten thousand. ¹¹ His head is purest gold; his hair is wavy and black as a raven. ¹² His eyes are like doves by the water streams, washed in milk, mounted like jewels. ¹³ His cheeks are like beds of spice yielding perfume. His lips are like lilies dripping with myrrh. ¹⁴ His arms are rods of gold set with topaz. His body is like polished ivory decorated with lapis lazuli. ¹⁵ His legs are pillars of marble set on bases of pure gold. His appearance is like Lebanon, choice as its cedars. ¹⁶ His mouth is sweetness itself; he is altogether lovely. This is my beloved, this is my friend, daughters of Jerusalem.

Although there are more scriptures referring to each other's body, I think you get the picture. This is about a couple fully engaged with each other. I love how he says, "You are altogether beautiful, my darling; there is no flaw in you." And she says, "His mouth is sweetness itself; he is altogether lovely. This is my beloved, this is my friend, daughters of Jerusalem."

Reflections
Fully engaged or low participation in sex or sexual intimacy are the results of the various kinds of initiation and response. These actions and reactions are sometimes done intentionally.
The following questions will help you examine your true intentions and level of engagement.

1. Are you fully engaged sexually in your marriage right now?
2. Before marriage, did you and your spouse talk about your likes/dislikes when it comes to sex?
3. Did you have premarital counseling and if so, was the topic of sex discussed?
4. Do you feel that sex is something that should be initiated by one spouse or the other?
5. What is your biggest takeaway from reading this chapter?

Prayer

Father, in Jesus name, please help me to be fully engaged sexually in my marriage. Help me to not be an observer but a full participant. Sexual intimacy between a husband and a wife is a beautiful thing that we can enjoy together. My body, nor my spouse's body has to be perfect. Help me to see my spouse's body as something of pure beauty and something to be desired because we belong to each other. And remembering that you made the body and what you made is good.

CHAPTER 4
ACCESSIBLE

Accessible- *able to be reached or entered*

Are you accessible to your spouse when it comes to sexual intimacy? Sometimes we get so busy with everyday life and life itself has its challenges. People often say, "I just don't have time to do everything I need to do." Some of us have children, jobs, business, ministry, etc. We have full lives and can easily get worn out and tired. Having an accessible heart is the starting point of being physically accessible to your spouse.

I believe in sexual intimacy. We should make time for each other and make it a priority. Have you noticed that throughout this book I haven't just said sex but, "sexual intimacy". Why? Because marital sex is truly about intimacy. About giving and receiving love through physical and sexual contact with your spouse. As stated before, sexual intimacy is very important and needs to be treated as a priority. I know some may say, "With everything that is going on in my life right now, I don't have time for regular sexual intimacy". I get it. I am not suggesting that I have never said this before.

For my husband and me, the more time we purposely make each other accessible to the other, the closer we get.

Being accessible sometimes means turning off the tv, muting the phone, and maybe going to bed early. Time is a precious commodity but look at it this way: According to the word of God, sexual intimacy is a need that only your wife or husband can righteously fill. You don't want to look back over your life and live with regrets. Spending time together is so important. I frequently think about the times I have spent with my husband and those times where we just cuddled and were close to each other. In those times we spent more nonsexual cuddle time together, just watching a movie, talking, and sharing our hearts. Some of us just need to slow down and make time to reflect on your life and what is important in this stage of your marriage right now.

Is it considered wrong to schedule sexual intimacy time? Sometimes the answer is "No it's not wrong" and other times more beneficial to do so. We schedule other things, why not schedule time to be together but also be open to quickies. A good quickie never hurt anyone (smile). How about starting out with an agreed upon time, day, place and then make every effort to keep the date. Learn to take full advantage of days off, holidays, vacations, quick overnight stays, etc.

Reflections

Again, in sexual intimacy, we should make time for each other. Honestly answer these questions to analyze how you prioritize time with your spouse.

1. Are you satisfied with the amount of time that you and your spouse spend together sexually?
2. Have you ever scheduled time to spend together?
3. As you get older, do you find that sex is not as important as it originally was?
4. Do you think about sex and make it a priority to be accessible for your spouse?
5. What is your biggest takeaway from reading this chapter?

Prayer

Father, in Jesus name help me to be more accessible to my spouse. Help me to understand that my heart condition is a big part of giving my spouse access to my body. Help me to prioritize our time of sexual intimacy. Help me to get the proper rest that I need and to take care of my body so that it is fully functional in every area. I desire to fully give myself to my spouse and not view it as an obligation but a blessing.

CHAPTER 5
KNOWLEDGEABLE

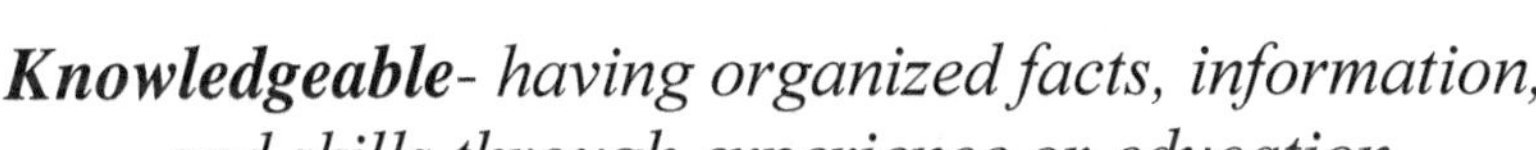

Knowledgeable- *having organized facts, information, and skills through experience or education*

So, years ago I worked with a company that sold romance products including accessories. We booked parties, conferences, workshops, bridal showers, etc. With this partnership I received a pamphlet about the products, how to host a party and how to demo the products. I also learned a lot about the human body, especially the sexual organs. Can I just tell you that the human body is a fascinating thing, and the sexual organs are incredible! The more knowledge that I gained as a sales/party rep, the more I became sexually free. I began to understand more about my body and my husband's body. I heard someone say that when you know better, you do better. I truly believe that God intended for us to really enjoy sexual intimacy and the more you know, the more you grow and the more you grow, the more you enjoy each other. This analogy explains how knowledge is power:

Years ago, I purchased a Jeep. I bought it from my husband, and he explained to me the cost, the features, etc. He explained the payments, etc. and some of the bells and whistles. There is no way that he could explain every feature of the vehicle at that time but the Jeep also came with an owner's manual which goes into more detail. Honestly, at that time I was more concerned with the monthly payment, gas, etc. I knew how to put it in drive, back it up, put in gas, etc. It wasn't until some random light came on that I even looked at the manual. Once I looked at the manual, I learned other things about my investment. My knowledge grew and I realized that there were a lot more features of this vehicle that I could have been enjoying. There was no difference in what it was created to do (get me from point A to B) but now with my acquired knowledge the ride was waaaaaaaay more enjoyable! Now I know what buttons to push, what warms me up, what cools me down. I understand that there are buttons to adjust just about everything in this Jeep!

I think you get exactly what I am saying. It stands to reason that since the human body is a single structure but made up of billions of smaller structures of cells, tissues, organs, and systems, there has got to be things that even the greatest minds don't know but are continually learning. As stated before, knowledge is power. Why not enjoy each other's body to the fullest?

The moral of the analogy: *"If you're gonna drive, why not let the drive be more enjoyable."* The sky is the limit. There is power in righteous agreement!

Here are just a few things that I read about the male and female sexual anatomy:

Female: Clitoris

- It is the pleasure center of the vulva.
- It has been said that pleasure is the main purpose of this organ.
- It becomes swollen when aroused.
- It is about 3 ½ to 4 ¼ inches long and about 2 ½ inches wide.
- It extends from about 7 to 13 centimeters into the body but only ¼ is visible.
- It has more than 10,000 nerve fibers enabling pleasurable sensations.
- Similar to the penis, it has glans, foreskin, and a shaft.
- 50-75 % of women need clitoral stimulation to achieve orgasm.

Male: Penis

- Most men have 3-5 erections every night mostly during rem sleep.
- The Glans penis, which is the head of the penis has the most nerve endings and is typically the most sensitive. It has about 6,000-8,000 nerve endings.
- The average length of a fully erect penis is 5.17 inches.
- Bigger isn't always better.
- There is no correlation between shoe size and penis size.
- The shaft, which is the biggest part of the penis, has fewer nerve endings but stimulating the shaft can move blood flow through the penis to the head which leads to orgasm.
- There are three parts to a penis and not all parts are visible externally.

I simply shared this information to encourage you to get to know your body and your spouse's body. It is great to get more knowledge about how things work and be able to get more enjoyment together. An expanded study on having knowledge about sex and sexual intimacy are in Part II of this book.

Reflections

How well do you know yourself and your spouse? Knowledge is a powerful change agent for improving your love life. The following questions are designed for self-reflection and conversation starters.

1. Have you and your spouse ever talked about how you feel about your body?
2. Have you ever discussed trying something new?
3. What does the term, "undefiled bed" mean to you?
4. Have you and your spouse discussed getting older and how that could impact changes in your body?
5. What is your biggest takeaway from reading this chapter?

Prayer

Father in Jesus name, help me to grow in knowledge concerning my body and my spouse's body. Help me to be more open to share my likes and dislikes in a safe environment with my spouse. Help me to not view sexual intimacy as something tawdry or dirty but something absolutely beautiful to be shared between a husband and wife.

Part II

Sexual Intimacy And The Test of Time

CHAPTER 6
GROWN FOLK TALK

At the time of this writing, my husband and I have been married for over 38 years. When I look back and think about the things we have been through and experienced. God has been good to us. We come from different backgrounds and have experienced a lot of things. I can safely say that I had no idea how much work would be involved to have a fulfilling marriage. As my husband says all the time, "Marriage is a dying to self". The longer you are married the more you realize that marriage is all about willing to go from "me to us", "mine to ours", being willing to make changes, and sometimes sacrifices for the sake of the team. I don't just want to grow old with him but also grow up with him. I don't want to keep making the same mistakes over and over. I want to be the best wife that I can be and hope that he will also put forth the effort to be the best husband that he can be.

Marriage is truly a process and not to be entered into lightly. Although this book is mainly about sexual intimacy, I felt that this chapter needed to be included because I feel that a lot of us entered marriage with some unrealistic expectations. Having someone to share your life with is a blessing but it does not mean that it is going to be easy. Marriage is work. Real work. My idea of marriage was that I would meet someone, fall in love, get married, have some kids and spend the rest of our lives together. Other than two hours of premarital counseling, I never talked to anyone about marriage and what to expect. We were told to share bank accounts, don't go to bed angry and that is all I remember. I know there were other things that were shared with us, but those two things really stood out to me.

I believe that God has anointed us to help other couples to maneuver through this journey called marriage. My husband and I have been blessed to officiate several marriage ceremonies and just like the couples themselves, every marriage ceremony was different. I love going to weddings because it is the beginning of two lives being joined together. I listen to the vows that are being stated, the love in the eyes of the bride and groom, the hopes, the dreams, the expectations…I remember my wedding day as I walked down the aisle in my beautiful white dress. I remember looking at my soon to be husband waiting for me along with our entire wedding party. It truly was a beautiful day. At that time we vowed to love, honor, obey, in sickness and in health, for richer or poorer, for better or worse. And at that time, we meant every word that we said. People change, life happens, vows get challenged and there are a lot of lessons learned. Here is what I have learned thus far:

- Marriage is a process, and you should be willing to change on a regular basis.
- You should have a TEAM mentality. This is something that I recently learned that opened my eyes wide open to what a team mentality looks like:

 My husband and I both love to bowl. Although in the past we had not gone a lot, every time we went, we truly enjoyed it. We are also both very competitive and like to win. As proof of our love for bowling and competitive nature, a couple of years ago a local bowling alley was offering a special on purchasing custom bowling balls. We decided to purchase them and most recently purchased bowling shoes. Also, in times past when we went bowling, I always wanted to beat my husband and would be happy if he got a gutter ball. As stated before, we are both competitive when it comes to bowling.

Recently, we decided to go bowling, but before we started, I suggested that we set a combined goal to see what our two scores together would average. I set a goal of 125. The first game we averaged 142 pts, second game 120 pts, third game 135 points and the 4th game 114. When we averaged all 4 games together, our combined score was 127.75, we surpassed our goal of 125. This is what happens when you allow the Holy Spirit to change your mindset from ME to US.

Here is what I learned from the change in our game that applies to marriage: 1. At the beginning we set a clear goal and realized that it would take both of us working together to make it happen. 2. Sometimes his score may be higher and mine lower and vice versa but it is about what the scores are together that makes the difference. 3. We are not competing against each other but with each other to accomplish the goal.
4. We celebrate each other's success and encourage each other when we don't reach the goal.
5. There may be times when one spouse is stronger than the other and that is perfectly fine.
6. We don't give up; we keep pressing forward and realize that we truly are better together.

- You should be willing to forgive and forgive some more.
- You should be willing to apologize and admit when you are wrong.
- You should be willing to sacrifice.

- Open communication is so very important.
- Love is a choice, and you should choose to love each day.
- Marriage is not 50/50. Our goal should be 100/100 but realize that due to circumstances and situations, those numbers will be lower. There is no perfect behavior and no perfect person so subsequently there is no perfect marriage.
- Marriage is not "give and take". It's "give and give" and praying that your spouse feels the same way.
- A relationship with God is a great foundation to build your marriage upon.
- Prayer is paramount and praying together is powerful.
- The more time I spend with God, the better wife I am to my husband.
- Understanding and speaking your spouse's love language is important.
- Having other couples in your life that are great examples of Godly marriages can enhance your marriage.

- Pre-marital counseling/coaching is very important and worth the time. I recommend it for at least 6 months.
- For followers of Jesus, marriage is just as much spiritual as it is natural. We need the Spirit of God to help, lead, and guide us into all truth.

That truth is not only about the word of God but also the truth about ourselves and those areas in our lives where we need to be better, do better, act better and allow our love to grow for each other.

CHAPTER 7
FOUR TYPES OF SEX

I thought this would be a fun chapter to add because sexual intimacy doesn't have to always be the same way, the same time, or the same place. I believe that you should be able to explore and be adventurous when it comes to making love with your spouse. The great thing about covenant sexual intimacy is that you are free to enjoy each other because you not only share the bed, but you also share your lives together. My husband recently made this statement, "Your home is your sanctuary, and your bedroom is your inner sanctuary". I absolutely loved that statement because I believe it to be true.

As stated before, I truly believe that God wants us to enjoy every aspect of our marriage. Sexual intimacy is a union of spirit, soul, and body. So, with that being said, I wanted to compare the types of meals to the types of sex. Everyone has to eat, and we don't all eat the same thing every day. Sometimes we go out and sometimes we prepare a meal at home. The key here is variety and I heard somewhere that variety is the spice of life.

The types of meals are described by their purpose, the amount of preparation time, how it is served, and in some examples the setting. Simultaneously, I've used similar terms for sex to describe its characteristics, planning (preparation time) and how those plans are implemented.

1. Fast Food

This type of meal was designed to "get it and go". You also have the option of getting it quicker by using the Drive-Thru. In sex, this "happy meal" is known as the Quickie.

- It requires no planning and no prep.
- It happens on the spur of the moment.
- It happens when the couple just wants to have a physical need met.
- There's not a lot of thought put into it.
- This or some other flirting scenario may occur: Your spouse walks by. You check him/her out. They look good. Your body responds.
- You could be thinking about a previous intimate time with your spouse, and you get aroused.
- Could be quick-hence the word quickie.

- Advantages:
  - It's fun.
  - It's spontaneous.
  - It's enjoyable.
  - And sometimes does not require a lot of time.
- But we all know, a lot of fast food is not ideal for maintaining a healthy body. 😊

Personal Story

I get a call from my husband while I was at work stating that he had locked his keys in the house. He was upset because he didn't want to have to bother me at work and also knew that I would be upset (Thank God that I have gotten better and not being upset when things happen). I admit that I was upset because I had to leave work. On the way home, I heard that still small voice inside telling me to not be upset and to do something that I would not normally do. I pulled in the driveway, he was standing at the door and began to apologize for locking the keys in the house. I said, "Okay alright, come on, let me give you some." The look on his face was pure shock. We had our quickie, I washed up and went back to work. End of the story.

2. Home Cooked

The purpose for home cooked meals is to provide an ordinary meal for any day. This kind of meal is enjoyed at home and usually prepared with some basic ingredients you already have. It involves more time and more care.

- They require some planning.
- It could be a pre-planned date night at home.
- It doesn't have to be fancy, but it could be something you have done before.
- It could be the same position, the same place, the same time.
- It could simply be that it has been a while, and you just miss each other and want to spend more quality time together.
- The emphasis here is on the planning, not just spur of the moment.

Personal Story

I planned a picnic in our family room. I put a comforter on the floor. We had shrimp cocktail and sparkling cider and then I gave my husband a lap dance.

3. Gourmet

Gourmet meals are extraordinary, and they are designed to increase the level of enjoyment. They require more complex preparation and they're made with special or exotic ingredients.

- More planning is involved.
- More time is spent together.
- Rested.
- The feeling is amorous.
- You've talked about how excited you are to do something different.
- You may have chosen the time to have the house to yourselves.
- Do a little something extra such as a back rub, a foot rub, etc.
- This could involve food, such as fresh fruit, whip cream, etc. as "appetizers".

4. Five Course

Course Meals are constructed for the full enjoyment of the meal from beginning to end. The goal is to give the consumer exhilarating and unique tasting experiences. The foods served are intentionally planned to complement one another. Courses are properly introduced with a short description and the presentation is always aesthetically pleasing.

- It is purposefully, slow and easy, so take your time.
- Have no other plans. It is just about the two of you.
  - *First Course*:
    - It requires lots of planning.
    - Advance preparations: clean sheets, clean bodies (taking showers together are wonderful), maybe some perfume, body butter, oils, etc.
    - Some nice sheet spray on your sheets may be used.
    - Have a clean, uncluttered bedroom.

  - *Second Course*:
    - Conversation-How much you love, need, and miss each other, how much you

- desire each other. What you plan to do with and to each other
- Express your desires to each other.

- o *Third Course:*
  - Flirting.
  - Playful kissing and touching may happen.
  - Lit candles to create the mood.

- o *Fourth Course*:
  - Listening to nice romantic music- I believe that every couple should have a nice playlist for love making.
  - Dancing, rubbing against each other: engaging in that type of dance that you should only do when it is just the two of you. This is where you can work, twerk, drop it like it's hot.

- o *Fifth Course:*
    - Do whatever you are in agreement with. For those of you who are believers, you know what is right.

    - All five senses are fully aroused: tasting, touching, smelling, seeing and hearing/listening.

    - You both are satisfied and express thankfulness and gratefulness because you are blessed to be able to be together and share your love together.

Note: Keep in mind, these are just some suggestions on how to build upon your sexual intimacy. The key here is to be willing to be adventurous and to simply love each other. Marital sexual intimacy is such a blessing and is best experienced willingly, openly and purposefully shared with each other. Listed on the next page are some things that my husband and I have done to enhance our relationship and intimate time.

- I took a pole dancing class. It was absolutely wonderful. It was not as easy as I thought it would be, but it was fun, and I learned a few moves.
- We have used products such as sheet spray, nipple cream, edible warming massage oil, etc.
- I purposely cook things that he loves to eat.
- My husband buys me flowers and has purchased my favorite candy and also my favorite perfume for no special occasion.
- I purchase 99% of his clothes from his favorite store.
- My husband gives me back rubs, foot rubs, and body massages.
- I gave my husband a lap dance.
- My husband surprised me with a five day vacation cruise.
- We have tried several different positions
- We have prayed together before being intimate.

CHAPTER 8
STAGES OF SEXUAL INTIMACY

My disclaimer here is that I am not saying that every couple goes through all of these stages. This is just some of my thoughts regarding my personal life and from others. Marriage is a process and therefore changes will occur within your relationship and within your body. Your desires, your expectations, your job, your family dynamics, your beliefs, amongst other things will change over the course of years.

Stage 1
Just the two of us
You're married and starting your new life together. You are back from the honeymoon where you were totally free to express your love to each other in wonderful ways. You were totally free to go and come as you please, no alarm clock, no time clock. You can stay up late, sleep in, and be amorous at any time.
Now you are back at home. The physical honeymoon may be over, but you are still enjoying your new life together and all the sexual pleasures that it brings. You are enjoying each other and the blessing of

sharing your life together. You get to see each other every day, go to bed together, wake up together, share meals, etc. But the real world sets back in and now it's time to get into a routine with work, bills, church, ministry, etc.

Stage 2
More than the two of us

You have now added some little blessings to your family. These little blessings are wonderful, but they come with added responsibilities. Now your time must be shared with others. Those first stages of parenthood can be rewarding and demanding all at the same time. Most couples go through tiredness, sleep deprivation and some mothers go through postpartum depression. Sexual intimacy may not be a high priority at this time, especially in the first few months after the baby is born. This is the time when open communication is so very important. With my first child I had a C-Section which takes quite a bit of time to heal afterwards. I remember going through so many different emotions, feeling the weight of knowing that we are now responsible for another life. For a lot of us the baby takes precedence over a lot of things. During this time, you have to learn to be flexible and realize that life as you know it has changed and therefore you have to be willing to change. You must be sure that you have realistic expectations of each other and keep the lines of communication open. For some women, during this time, non-sexual touch is so important, such as back rubs, foot rubs, massages, etc. It's a way of showing physical love but not expecting anything in return.

Stage 3
Life becomes more hectic
The kids are growing up and this means homework, after school activities, doctor appointments, and you can find yourselves having less and less time for intimacy. In addition to this are the continuous responsibilities of maintaining a household, working, paying bills, extended family time, and just trying to have a peaceful home where everyone works well together. This time, as stated before, is a great time to keep the lines of communication open. Try to schedule date nights and do some "check ins". How are you? How do you feel right now? This may be a good time to purposefully schedule some husband and wife time so that you don't allow "husband and wife" to get lost in being" mom and dad". I know it can be easier said than done.

We must remember that in your family, the foundation was built by husband and wife. Everything and everyone else was added on to the foundation. Sexual intimacy is that time when you are connecting spirit, soul, and body. You may find that the more time you focus on this and making this time a priority, the more you will be connected. In addition to that, you will be able to better navigate the rest of your married lives together because you are a united front. It is something so very special when you can learn to focus on each other even though you have others to consider. Remember this, the kids will one day grow up and leave. Then you will be back to the first stage but now you are more mature and ready to reap the rewards of continuing to take care of each other while living the "family" life.

Stage 4
Back to where you started
The kids are out of the house and it's just the two of you again. This can be a time where you go back to focusing completely on the two of you. You are older, wiser, and getting settled in your new life of focusing on being husband and wife again. You are still parents/grandparents but now you have more time to travel, experience life, and enjoy complete sexual freedom again. You can go back to running around the house naked, experiencing quickies whenever you want to, trying new positions, new places, etc. However, even in the midst of all this freedom, as we get older our bodies change and some things may not feel the same way they once did. You may have more physical

limitations and some health concerns. For example, for women, there is menopause. I jokingly said that menopause is when wives put their men on pause (get it?). This is definitely a time for open communication to discuss the changes your bodies are experiencing and realizing that we may need to adjust our expectations of each other. Again, sexual intimacy is something to be enjoyed, not endured. The more transparent you are with your spouse, the better you will be. This also is a great time to be more creative, like adding more touching, holding hands, back rubs, foot rubs, playful flirting, maybe even adding some other things like sheet spray, nipple cream, warming massage oil.

Personal Story

We are in stage 4 now. I truly feel that I love my husband now more than I ever have. We are learning to truly work together and be good to each other even more. We love the intimacy that being together for a long time can bring. Because it is just the two of us at home now, we spend a lot of time together. We get to make decisions based on our needs and desires for just the two of us. As stated earlier, your bodies go through changes as you age but that does not mean that you can't still have fulfilled sexual intimacy. As I write this book, I am menopausal and have been very open with my husband about it. He understands and prays for me, and I appreciate the prayers so very much, We respect each other's body and try to make sexual intimacy a priority and can just lay in bed after being intimate, just simply laughing and talking and enjoying being together sexually, physically, mentally, emotionally and especially spiritually. Remember, according to the Word of God, the marriage bed is undefiled.

CHAPTER 9
INTERVIEW WITH MY BEST FRIEND

For this chapter, I decided to interview my husband, Ray. I wanted his input, and I also wanted him to have a chapter in the book. He has been such a tremendous blessing in my life in the 40 years that I have known him. He prays for me, challenges me, and encourages me to be who God created me to be. He has also gained a lot of wisdom when it comes to marriage and especially according to the Word of God. Ray takes his role as a husband very seriously and I have watched him grow in this area. He always says, "Marriage is a dying to self."

Question 1: So, far what is the greatest lesson you have learned about marriage?

Response: *It's about the sacrifice that it takes to have a great marriage. It's dying to yourself and seeing the results of that. When you appreciate the efforts that I make to have a happy home and to have a great marriage and when I see the happiness and the joy on your face, it means the world to me. I am grateful to have the opportunity that I have to be married as long* *as I have been married. It has had its' tremendous ups, and it has had its' downs. I am grateful for the time that we have had together. I think the greatest lesson is the sacrificing and laying down my life for the good of the marriage. It means a lot to me and I really appreciate that you appreciate my sacrifice. And even though I can say it is a sacrifice, this is what a man is supposed to do. He is supposed to lay down his ego for the good of the marriage. I am thankful that I have been there for you to be the emotional and the physical support that you need. I am greatly honored that I have been able to do this and will continue to do so.*

Question 2: Has our marriage been what you thought it would be?

Response: *It is both yes and no. In my immaturity, I was expecting more things for myself out of the marriage and when I didn't get those things, they became areas of contention. But on the other hand, marriage has been better than what I thought it was going to be. For example, when I was giving and the giving was appreciated it caused me to want to continue to give. As long as I was not a taker but a giver, marriage became more than I expected it to be.*

Question 3: What do you think a wife's role is in the marriage?

Response: *The wife is a helper and you certainly are. It's not that you are beneath me or above me but beside be. What I don't see, you see. It is the perspective that you bring that a lot of times helps me to see things more clearly. I think that God created the woman to be the helper because you see things that I may not be able to see, You are wise and see things different from me and I have to respect that you are gonna see things different from me. And I have to be willing to listen to what you have to say. That means a lot in the marriage to have the two work together and work things out. We are better together than as an individual. God did not intend for men to do life by themselves no matter what level they are trying to get to. We are not meant to go up there by ourselves. We (speaking about our marriage) are meant to climb together, to need each other. The higher we are able to climb is based on my willingness to listen to what you are saying to help get us to that next level.*

Question 4: If you had to do it all over again, what would you do different?

Response: *I don't know if I would do anything different. Believe it or not, I don't know if I would do* *anything different because everything that has been accomplished has been woven all together to get me to where I am today. Sometimes there are things that you regret. There are times of remorse and times of repentance, but it's all part of the tapestry. It's like the story you told about the man who visited a shop where students were making tapestries. As the man was walking around the room with the instructor and noticed that there were cases where the students made mistakes, but they did not cut out the mistakes. They basically worked around them and they became a beautiful part of the tapestry. It is the same thing with our lives. There have been times that I have made bad decisions and there has been times that I have done and said things but nevertheless, I don't think I would change anything because it made me the man who I am and I am grateful to God for the man that I am and the man I am yet to become.*

Question 5: Was there a time when you felt like walking away from the marriage?

Response: *No. There were times where you got on my nerves, but I never felt like walking away. I never felt like quitting because of my background and because* *of my athletic background and my experiences as a child. I felt like something had to change somehow or another, but I was determined that the change would have to come from me. I just never felt like quitting as I said before regarding my athletic background.*

There is one thing that people don't understand about sports is that at some point in time, I don't care how good you are, you are gonna lose and you are gonna have your rear end handed to you. It's just a matter of time. So, it's going to happen, but you just don't quit. Eventually the tables will turn, you just need to hang in there. The impending result is a great marriage that continues to get better.

Question 6: How important is the word of God in marriage?

Response: *It is very important. We have to look at the one who instituted marriage in the first place. We have to look at what the word of God says and how we are to conduct ourselves as husband and wives, as believers as it describes to us our relationship one with another. The scripture tells us to love God and to love our neighbor as we love ourselves and, in my opinion, your first neighbor is your spouse. You are the first person I need to love, and it goes back to the word of God. How well do I treat my neighbor? Not the person* *next door to me but the person that was my neighbor from afar but is now my neighbor in my same household. I have to treat you well long before I walk out the door.*

Question 7: Do you know my love languages and if you do, how do you speak them?

Response: *Your love languages are quality time and physical touch. I have to practice on a regular basis and be willing to do on a consistent basis. This is a part of love. These are not my love languages, but they are yours and I need to make them a priority because they are important to you. Even though there are times that I may not necessarily feel like I want to do this but it is important to you.*

Question 8: How do you feel about me writing this book and what did you think about the title, *Sanctified F.R.E.A.K.*

Response: *It's a great book. It's something that we have been told that we needed to do and you are the right person doing it. You are a little more detailed oriented than I am even though you don't think you are. I think it is a good book. I believe that it is going to help marriages and bring a good perspective, not only from the bedroom perspective but also from* *everyday aspect of being able to communicate with one another and being able to do the things that make the bedroom experience a lot more pleasing and pleasurable not just for one but for both spouses.*

Question 9: How important is sex to a man?

Response: *To a man, it is something that he thinks about quite often. I am not going to say that it consumes him, but most of us think about sex often. I think a lot of times, we think about it so much we think about how to get more and we do things to try to get our needs met but it should not become an idol. It is important but the relationship is more important than just the sexual aspect of the relationship.*

Question 10: Do you pray with me and is it important that you pray with me?

Response: *Yes, I do pray with you and I also pray by myself. In times past I thought that praying by myself was good but now realize the importance of praying with you and with our children. I continue to pray and I think the greatest thing that has occurred over the last few years is praying with you just about every day. Prayer is so much more powerful when we pray together. I look forward to us praying together and it is an honor to have a prayer partner. I think a man* *should have a prayer life apart from his wife but praying together is equally important.*

Question 11: How do you feel about the statement in the bible that says that the husband is the head of the wife? Do you feel that this is an honor for the husband?

Response*: I think that it is an honor but also it is quite a challenge too. Once you begin to study the Word of God and you see what the responsibility of being a man really is, it is not for me to "Lord authority" over you but to lead and to lead by example. That is a huge responsibility and I have to make sure that I stick as close as possible to the manual (the Bible) to see how to lead properly. I don't want to mislead and be a bad example of a leader. One thing that we have at our church is a men's conference call and one of the things that our Elder taught from the 2ⁿᵈ chapter of Titus is how the older men should be an example to the younger men and how the younger men should conduct themselves. So as men, whether young or old, we are making an impression and held accountable to a standard. That means that I need to carry myself in such a way that a younger man would want to model his life after me. In the bible the Apostle Paul says, "Follow me as I follow Christ" and that is a huge statement to be said. I need to carry myself in such a* *way that any man would want to treat their wife in a respectful and honorable way as they see me and the way I carry myself, that they would want to do the same for their wife. So, it is an honor but it also a challenge!*

Question 12: Growing up, were there men in your family that you were able to learn from about being a good husband?

Response: *The greatest lesson that I learned from watching my father and stepmother and my aunt and uncle(who raised me) was how to stay together. Although they had their challenges, they stuck it out. In both cases, both couples were married until they passed away, They never left each other.*

Question 13: If you had the opportunity to talk to some young men, what would you tell them to do while they are single to prepare for being married?

Response: *I think that I would tell them to prepare themselves now to be a good person to your wife. If you are practicing doing good things now, continue to do those things. A lot of times as men we feel that we've gotten what we have tried to accomplish. We tend to let up. Don't ever let up but continue to do what* *you know is right. Prepare yourself financially. It is not just about the amount of money you make but also saving properly, spending properly, and that you are not over extended. You also need to be sure that you are not carrying a lot of debt and to be wise with your money. I also recommend getting counseling from older men.*

Question 14: In regard to finances, have we had any challenges and who's responsible for the finances in the family?

Response: *We have had our challenges but I think over time as we have worked together, we have been able to overcome those challenges. I feel that it is the husband's responsibility when it comes to the finances but in today's society, due to dual incomes things have changed a bit. The finances that are coming in have to be managed properly regardless of who is making what. I believe that it is the man's responsibility to work and provide for his family and to do the best he can. The bible says that if a man will not work, he should not eat. As a man we have to do our part and hang in there. I know for a man, sometimes it can be discouraging not being able to provide everything that is needed. Sometimes men feel insufficient, you feel that you are a failure. That is why it is so important for a wife to support her husband and not tear him down.*

A man's ego is delicate and if he feels that his effort is not appreciated it causes him to retreat. As men, we have to make sure that we do the best we can, and it is appreciated. Once it is appreciated, it will cause us to want to do more. One thing for sure, in our struggles at one time I had three jobs, and you never diminished the fact that I had three jobs and you appreciated the effort. Even when I had one job getting paid by commission and I did not get the check amount we needed, you talked to God, and you didn't complain to me and somehow God made it all work out. It is such a big thing to have the woman with you, that helpmate. that is what she is there for, and you work together.

Question 15: There is a scripture that says for husbands to love their wives and wives to respect their husband, what have I done to make you feel respected? What do you do to make me feel loved?

Response: *Listening to me is one of the biggest things that you do. You appreciate the efforts that I make and to me that is respect. You don't take things for granted and you have said that you have had to work at not taking me for granted and that it has not come easy. Love is laying down your life on a regular basis, it's not just a one time thing. A husband is supposed to love his wife over and over. It's not just providing for her financially or materially but also emotionally. Being* *able to listen to her and talk to her on a regular basis and not just going out and conquering but being able to be there emotionally for her.*

CHAPTER 10
MY TESTIMONY

When I tell you that God has done an amazing work in me, it is not an exaggeration. I am a wife, mother, grandmother, an associate pastor, a member of several women's groups, a leader but most important, I am a follower and a disciple of Jesus Christ. I would have never thought in a million years that I would have written a book entitled, *Sanctified F.R.EA.K.*

I have often heard people say that to fully understand my passion, you have to understand my pain. God has been good to me and blessed me with a wonderful husband who loves me and has loved me through all of my "stuff". At the printing of this book, I have been married over 38 years. As in any marriage, we have had our share of ups and downs mainly in finances and sexual intimacy. I admit that I was not a virgin when I married my husband. I had had previous sexual experiences, but I am no longer ashamed because of what Jesus did on the cross for me. I am a new woman in Christ and according to Psalm 34: 4-5

I have sought the Lord, and He answered me: He delivered me from all my fears. Those who look to him are radiant; their faces are never covered with shame.

The first time my husband and I were physically intimate was our wedding night. I must admit that we while dating, had some intimate moments (petting, kissing, etc.) Due to the fact that both of us were believers at the time, we made the decision to wait until our wedding night to be sexually intimate. Can I tell you that it was very, very hard to wait prior to marriage because we were both very attracted to each other and our bodies definitely desired each other.

Let's fast forward to the first year of our marriage. Although we were happy something was not quite right for me. I loved my husband dearly and he loved me dearly but I was not sexually free and did not get full understanding of marital sexual intimacy until much later in our marriage. I was never taught about sexual intimacy and although I had sex before marriage it was about a feeling and not love between a husband and wife. I loved God and I loved my husband and I wanted to enjoy both to the fullest. I wanted to love God more by also loving his son (my husband) the way he deserved to be loved and to be respected.

We sought counseling with one of the associate pastors at our church which set us on the path to where we are now. He helped me to understand that the things of the past were in the past. Not everything was my fault and God had set me free from past sins, hurts, etc. I apologized to my husband for withholding myself (body and soul) from him, picking fights so that I did not have to have sex and trying to make him feel guilty for wanting me and that thinking that my body belonged to me only.

I am a work in progress and because of my love for God and all that he has done for me, how he has set me free, how he loves me unconditionally, I work at being spontaneous and free in the bedroom. I have grown in sexual intimacy and being giving, receptive and accessible to my husband. I thank God that after 38 years of marriage, I still desire my husband and he desires me. Our desire is to not only grow old together but to also grow up together in every area of our lives.

Our call is to help married couples experience all the greatness that God has for them in every area of their marriage including sexual intimacy. So, you see, there is nothing wrong and everything right about being Freaky in the bedroom!!!

My prayer is that as you have read this book, you will let go of the past and be free to be who God created you to be in the area of sexual intimacy in your marriage. Marriage is a wonderful thing and I truly believe that God wants you to enjoy every area of your marriage. Sexual intimacy is more than just the physical act of sexual intercourse but also enjoying the unity and oneness as you share your spirit, soul, and body.

ABOUT THE AUTHOR

Vicki Tyler Waters, ThD

Dr. Vicki Tyler Waters, founder of Woman to Woman Ministries, (2010) is an inspirational speaker, instructor, counselor, entrepreneur, and friend to thousands of women along the east coast of the United States. She has ministered at several women's conferences for married and single women. Dr. Waters has been a key team player on many ministry teams for women, married couples, youth, community outreach, deliverance ministry, prayer, and missions. For over 20 years, she and her husband, Dr. Ray Waters, have faithfully served as deacons and elders at Lighthouse Christian Center, Highland Springs, Virginia.

H.E.A.L.T.H. & W.E.A.L.T.H. Ministries, a ministry for husbands and wives, were founded by the Waters. They have been guest speakers at several churches and conferences sharing about the importance of marriage and family. Their ministry is streamed live on Facebook. Presently, the Waters are serving as Associate Pastors and continue to travel across the United States encouraging and equipping couples for successful marriages.